TOASTS
AND GRACES

CHARLES MacLEAN
ILLUSTRATED BY CATHERINE McWILLIAMS

Appletree Press

First published in 1993 by
The Appletree Press Ltd,
The Old Potato Station,
14 Howard Street South,
Belfast BT7 1AP
Tel: +44 (0) 28 90 243074
Fax: +44 (0) 28 90 246756
E-mail: frontdesk@appletree.ie
Web Site: www.appletree.ie

A Little Book of Scottish Toasts and Graces

A catalogue reference for this book is
available from The British Library.

ISBN 0-86281-394-8

9 8 7 6 5 4 3

This book is for Alexander McCall Smith,
scholar, story-teller, saxophonist and author of
The Criminal Law of Botswana

Introduction

Before humans drank the health of the living, they drank the *minni* of the dead or of the gods. *Minni* is Old Norse and means "love, memory and thought of the absent one" all at the same time. With Christians it became "God s *minni*"; in medieval times there were "*minnying*" or "*mynde*" days, and even today Scots use the verb "*mind*" rather than "remember".

Drinking the health of the living was closely associated with *minnying*. Greeks and Romans drank to one another; Goths pledged each other with *hails* ("health") and Saxons with *waes hael* ("be in health").

It was a Saxon, Margaret "Atheling", great-niece of King Edward the Confessor and wife of the Scottish King Malcolm Canmore, who first introduced the "grace cup" as a means of inducing the restless Scots to remain at table until grace had been said at the end of the meal. Queen Margaret, who arrived in Scotland in about 1069 (after being driven out of England by the Norman Conquest) was so devout she was canonised. She arranged that a cup of the finest available wine should be passed round, but only after grace had been said.

In this context, "grace" means "giving thanks". The custom of saying grace either before or after a meal was widely practised by the Jews, Greeks and Romans and adopted universally by Christians, who often commenced with the words *Gratias Deo agamus* ("let us give thanks to God"), a formula which originated in monastic refectories.

While on the subject of word origins, the commonest toast of all, "cheers", entered the English language in the thirteenth century via the Anglo-Norman *chere*, meaning "face", and derives from the Latin *cara*. "Face" quickly became a metaphor for the state of the mind behind it, hence "be of good cheer", "be cheerful", "cheers".

The origin of making "toasts" is more obscure. The word derives from the Vulgar Latin *tostare* (to scorch or roast). From Classical times is was common to flavour wine by floating small pieces of toasted bread in it. Sometimes these sippets would be flavoured with spices; at other times the carbon alone would mellow the wine. It is supposed that the drinking of "toasts" derives from the gallantry that "the name of the lady (to whom one was drinking) enhanced the drink more than any toast". This usage first appears in the seventeenth century.

Sir Richard Steele explained the practice of drinking toasts in the *Tatler*, June 4th 1709, recalling an event that had taken place at Bath some thirty years before:

> *"It happened that on a publick day a celebrated beauty of those times was in the cross bath, and one of the crowd of her admirers took a glass of the water in which the fair one stood, and drank her health to the company. There was in the place a gay fellow, half fuddled, who offered to jump in, and swore, though he liked not the liquor, he would have the toast. He was opposed in his resolution; yet this whim gave foundation to the present honour which is done to the lady we mention in our liquor, who has ever since been called a toast."*

In Scotland, during the eighteenth century, toasting was all the rage — at every level of society. The custom was frequently used as an excuse for intemperate drinking, or as a way of compelling guests to drink. Each time the glasses were filled, someone was called upon to make a toast (or "sentiment", as they were also called). Often the toast-maker would insist that the toast must be emphasised by drinking a "bumper" (i.e. draining the glass). He would then call upon the next to make a toast, or if he had toasted somebody present, they would rise, reply and toast another. Often the rounds of toasts went on for some time: when George IV visited Edinburgh in August 1822, forty-seven toasts were pronounced at the banquet in his honour!

In his *Memorials Of My Time*, published in the 1850s, Lord Cockburn, the eminent Scottish judge, remembers:

> "After dinner, and before the ladies retired, there generally began what was called 'Rounds' of toasts, when each gentleman named an absent lady, and each lady an absent gentleman, and the persons named were toasted, generally with allusions and jokes about the fitness of the union. And worst of all there were 'Sentiments'. These were short epigramatic sentences expressive of moral feelings and virtues, and were thought refined and elegant productions ... The conceited, the ready, or the reckless, hackneyed in the art, had a knack of making new sentiments applicable to passing incidents with great ease. But it was a dreadful oppression on the timid or the awkward."

Elsewhere he recalls:

"Every glass during dinner had to be dedicated to some one. It was thought sottish and rude to take wine without this, as if forsooth there was nobody present worth drinking with. I was present about 1803 when the late Duke of Buccleuch took a glass of sherry by himself at the table of Charles Hope, then Lord Advocate, and this was noticed afterwards as a piece of direct contempt."

"Rounds" often went on until the company fell unconscious beneath the table. Dean Ramsay, in his *Reminiscences of Scottish Life and Character* (1857), recounts an incident which had been told him by Duncan Mackenzie, a celebrated author of the early nineteenth century:

"He had been involved in a regular drinking party. He was keeping as free from the usual excesses as he was able, and as he marked companions around him falling victims to the power of drink, he himself dropped off under the table amongst the slain, as a measure of precaution, and lying there, his attention was called to a small pair of hands working at his throat; on asking what it was, a voice replied, "Sir, I'm the lad that's to lowse the neck-cloths" (i.e. to untie the cravats of the guests and prevent apoplexy or suffocation)".

And again:

"There had been a carousing party at Castle Grant, many years ago, and as the evening advanced towards morning, two Highlanders were in attendance to carry the guests upstairs, it being understood that none could by any other means arrive at their sleeping apartments. One or two of the guests, whether

from their abstinence or their superior strength of head, were walking upstairs, and declined the proffered assistance. The attendants were astonished, and indignantly exclaimed, "Ach, it's sare cheenged times at Castle Grant, when gentlemens can gang to bed on their ain feet"! "

Not surprising, then, that the Golden Age for Scottish toasts are the eighteenth and early nineteenth centuries. This little book contains many examples. But toasts are continually being invented, updated, personalised, and it is to be hoped that, as well as being a repository of examples of a curious human activity, *Scottish Toasts* might inspire its readers to create their own toasts, in the knowledge that they are continuing a convivial tradition which stretches back at least three hundred years.

The Selkirk Grace

Some hae meat, and canna eat,
And some wad eat that want it;
But we hae meat, and we can eat —
And sae the Lord be thankit.

Robert Burns

This grace takes its name from a person, Dunbar Douglas, 4th Earl of Selkirk, rather than the town in the Scottish Borders.

In fact, Robert Burns only visited Selkirk once. He was touring with a companion, and arrived at Selkirk on Sunday 13th May 1787. It was raining hard, so they took shelter in Veitch s Inn, where the local doctor and two friends were sitting by the fire. The innkeeper asked if the strangers could join them, but the doctor refused, on the grounds that 'they did not look like gentlemen'.

Three days later, Dr Clarkson learned who the stranger was: a contemporary, James Hogg, wrote that "his refusal [to allow them to join him] hangs about the doctor's heart like a dead weight to this day, and will do 'til the day of his death, for the bard had no more enthusiastic an admirer."

The grace itself was probably first delivered at the Heid Inn in Kirkcudbright High Street, in the presence of Lord Selkirk, in July 1794 (the inn is now named the Selkirk Arms). It is also possible that this, Burns' most famous toast, was traditional, and not in fact composed by him after all. He certainly never wrote it down.

Address to a Haggis

Fair fa' your honest, sonsie face,
Great chieftain o' the pudding-race!
Aboon them a' ye tak your place,
    Painch, tripe or thairm;
Weel are ye wordy o' a grace
    As lang's my arm.

Ye Pow'rs wha mak mankind your care,
And dish them out their bill o' fare,
Auld Scotland wants nae skinking ware
    That jaups in luggies;
But, if ye wish her gratefu' prayer,
    Gie her a haggis!

Robert Burns

(*Fair fa'* — 'may good befall'; *sonsie* — comely, jolly; *aboon*—
above; *painch* — paunch, stomach; *thairm* — intestines; *wordy* —
worthy; *skinking ware* — slops, thin liquid stuff; *that joups in
luggies* — slops around in pails (or two handed bowls))

Haggis was not well known to Burns and, when he was invited
to attend an annual harvest supper in 1785 at which a sheep's
haggis was traditionally eaten, he wrote the poem in advance:
"Everyone thought the grace was extempore, but the Poet
himself told them he came prepared for the Haggis but not for
the (large) company present" (Grierson). The extract above
is the first and last of eight verses.

The Poet's Graces

(Before the meal)

> *O Thou who kindly dost provide*
> *For every creature's want!*
> *We bless Thee, God of Nature wide,*
> *For all thy goodness lent.*
> *And, if it please Thee, heavenly Guide,*
> *May never worse be sent;*
> *But, whether granted or denied,*
> *Lord bless us with content.*

(After the meal)

> *O Thou, in whom we live and move,*
> *Who made the sea and shore;*
> *Thy goodness constantly we prove,*
> *And grateful would adore;*
> *And, if it please Thee, Power above!*
> *Still grant us with such store*
> *The friend we trust, the fair we love,*
> *And we desire no more.*

Robert Burns

These graces were made extempore, and were first published in the *Edinburgh Courant* in August 1789. In more recent times they have become known as "The Poet's Graces".

At the Globe Tavern

(Grace Before Meat)

> *O Lord, when hunger pinches sore,*
> *Do Thou stand us in stead,*
> *And send us, from Thy bounteous store,*
> *A tup — or wether-head!*

(Grace After Meat)

> *O Lord, since we have feasted thus,*
> *Which we so little merit,*
> *Let Meg now take the flesh away,*
> *And Jock bring in the spirit!*

(From *There was a Lass, they ca'd her Meg*)

> *A man may drink and no be drunk;*
> *A man may fight and no be slain;*
> *A man may kiss a bonnie lass,*
> *And aye be welcome back again.*

Robert Burns

(*tup* — a young ram; *wether-head* — a sheep's head)

The Globe Tavern in Tarbolton, Ayrshire, was one of Burns'
haunts. An early (1801) version of *Grace After Meat* has "Let
William Hislop bring the spirit" as its concluding line — Hislop
was the landlord. "Meg" and "Jock" were variations for
different occasions.

Scotch Drink

Freedom and Whisky gang thegither –
Tak aff your dram!

Robert Burns

Burns was fond of whisky although, at the time he wrote, it was not as generally available in the Lowlands as it is today. This is one of his most quoted "bumper" toasts.

The following preface to Burns' poem *Scotch Drink* was inspired by Proverbs xxxi: 6—7: "Give strong drink to the desperate and wine to the embittered; such men will drink and forget their poverty and remember their trouble no longer". The poem was written during the winter 1785 1786.

Gie him strong drink until he wink,
That's sinking in despair;
An' liquor guid to fire his bluid,
That's prest wi' grief an' care:
There let him bowse, and deep carouse,
Wi' bumpers flowing o'er,
Till he forgets his loves or debts
An' minds his griefs no more.

Here's A Bottle

Here's a bottle and an honest man!
What wad ye wish for mair, man?
Wha kens, before his life may end,
What his share may be o' care, man?

Then catch the moments as they fly,
And use them as ye ought, man.
Believe me happiness is shy,
And comes not aye when sought, man!

Robert Burns

(*mair* — more; *wha* — who; *kens* — knows)

This first appears in a MS of 1808. The sentiment was echoed by William Blake in his famous "Gnomic" verse:

'He who bends to himself a Joy
Doth the winged life destroy;
But he who kisses the Joy as it flies
Lives in Eternity's sunrise.'

O Fortuna!

When we're gaun up the hill o' Fortune,
May we ne're meet a frien' comin' doun!

May puirtith ne'er throw us in the mire,
or gowd in the high saddle

Dean Ramsay

(*puirtith* — poverty; *mire* — mud; *gowd* — gold)

"Fortune" — good and bad — was even more acutely felt by our forefathers than by us today. So it is not surprising that so many toasts were devoted to it. Dean Ramsay (1793—1872), was an Episcopalian clergyman in Edinburgh. In *Reminiscences of Scottish Life and Character* (published in 1858, went into twenty-one editions during its author's lifetime, and was described by Sydney Smith as "one of the best answers to the charge of want of humour in the Scots") he lists several prosaic examples, including:

May the honest heart ne'er feel distress

May the winds of adversity ne'er blow in your door

An earlier, and monumental, work entitled *A Complete Collection of Scottish Proverbs* (James Kelly M.A.; London, 1721) includes the charming toast:

Better the heid o'the yeomanry than the arse o'the gentry!

24

Here's Tae Us ...

Here's tae us –
Wha's like us –
Damn few,
And they're a' deid –
Mair's the pity!

(i.e. 'Here's to us and those like us — there aren't many, and those that were are all dead. More's the pity!')

This "Golden Age" toast is still common today in Scotland. Solidarity amongst topers is another familiar theme of toasting through the ages:

Here's to them that lo'es us, or lends us a lift!

May ye ne'er want a frien' or a dram to gie him

May we be happy and our enemies know it!

Here's to them that like us –
Them that think us swell –
And here's tae them that hate us –
Let's pray for them as well.

— and, of course, the famous (and still current) Edinburgh toast:

'Lang may yer lum reek –
Wi' ither folks coal!'

(*lum reek* — chimney smoke)

Health, Wealth and Happiness

Here's health to the sick,
Stilts to the lame,
Claes to the back,
And brose to the wame!

(*claes* — clothes; *brose* — soup, drink; *wame* — stomach)

Variations include:

May ye aye be happy,
And ne'er drink from a toom cappie!

(*toom cappie* — empty bowl)

The ingle-neuk, wi'routh o' bannocks and bairns

(i.e. The corner by the fire, with plenty of oat-cakes and children)

May we a' be canty and cosy,
And ilk hae a wife in his bosy!

(*canty* — lively; *ilk* — each; *bosy* — bosom)

Or simply:

Thumping luck and fat weans!

(*weans* — children)

There's Nae Luck aboot the Hoose ...

*May the best ye've ever seen
Be the worst ye'll ever see;
May a moose ne'er leave yer girnal
Wi' a tear drap in his ee.
May ye aye keep hale and he'erty
Till ye're auld enough tae dee,
May ye aye be juist as happy
As I wish ye aye tae be.*

(*moose* — mouse; *girnal* — meal chest)

This toast might be termed "transitional". The first two lines are traditional, and often quoted (by Dean Ramsay among others), but this full version has the sentimentality of the nineteenth-century music hall.

Hi-jinks

Good wine, a friend, or being dry —
Or lest you should be bye and bye —
Or any other reason why.

Allan Ramsay

"Hi-jinks. A drunken game, or new project to drink and be rich" begins the distinguished poet Allan Ramsay (1686—1758) in describing this popular Scottish pastime.

Once the glass is filled to the brim, one of the company takes a pair of dice, cries "Hi-jinks" and rolls them. The number cast indicates who must drink the bumper, or pay a forfeit if he declines (in which case he cries "Hi-jinks" and throws again, to choose another). If he chooses to drink he takes whatever is in the kitty, but only if he fulfills the procedure exactly: drinks the bumper; sweeps up the money; fills the glass to the brim; cries "Hi-jinks"; and counts the numbers of the dice correctly.

Ramsay concludes: "A rare project this, and no bubble I can assure you: for a covetous fellow may save money, and get himself as drunk as he can desire in less than an hour s time".

The Bon Accord

Blythe to meet,
Wae to part,
Blythe to meet aince mair.

(i.e. Happy to meet, sorrowful to part, happy to meet once
more)

Guid nicht to ye, and tak yer nappie:
A willie-waught's a guid nicht-cappie!

(i.e. Good night to you, and drink up your ale —
A friendly drink's a good night-cap)

Blythe, blythe aroun' the nappie
Let us join in social glee:
While we're here we'll hae a drappie —
Scotia's sons have aye been free!

(*nappie* — strong ale; *aye* — always)

These toasts come from the North-east of Scotland. The first
is known as "The Bon-Accord Toast". *Bon Accord* is the motto
of the City of Aberdeen, and originated in 1308, when the
citizens of the town rose up one night in a sudden and secret
insurrection, massacred the (English) garrison in the castle and
seized the town for Robert the Bruce. "Bon-Accord" was the
watchword they adopted during the operation.

The Great Toast

Suas i, suas i;
Seas i, seas i;
A'nall i, a'nall i;
A'null i, a'null i.
Na h'uile la gu math diut, mo charaid.
Sguab as i!
Agus cha n'ol neach eile as a ghloine so gu brath!

Up with it, up with it;
Down with it, down with it;
Over to you; over to you
Over to me; over to me.
May all your days be good, my friend.
Drink it up!
And let no one ever drink from this glass again!

This toast is properly drunk standing on a chair, with one foot
on the table. The glass is raised and lowered, brought in and
out, with each line, drained on the words *Sguab as i,* and
smashed at the end.

A charming variant is:

Neither above you,
Nor below you –
Always with you

The Toast Master's Companion

May opinion never float on the waves of ignorance

May we look forward with pleasure, and backwards without remorse

May we never crack a joke to break a reputation

May we never suffer for principles we do not hold

To the man that feels for sorrows not his own

Great men honest, and honest men great

May we live to learn and learn to live well

May we live in pleasure and die out of debt

A head to earn and a heart to spend

Health of body, peace of mind, a clean shirt and a guinea

The Toastmaster's Companion was published in Stirling in 1822 — the year George IV visited Edinburgh (see p. 7) — and provides a useful insight into the topics that interested the drinking classes at that time.

Well Met!

Here's our noble sel's, weel met the day!

Robert Fergusson

The poet Robert Fergusson (1750—1774) was born in Edinburgh, of humble parents (his father was a draper's clerk) but soon moved to Dundee, where he won a scholarship to the Grammar School and later to St. Andrews University. Here he distinguished himself both as a student of science and for his high-spirited, hard-living and impulsive character.

Fergusson was greatly admired by Robert Burns. In one poem he celebrates the "Daft Days" between Christmas and the first Monday of the New Year. Here are the last two verses.

And thou, great god of Aqua Vitae!
Wha sways the empire of this city,
Where fou we're sometimes capernoity,
Be thou prepar'd
To hedge us frae that black banditti,
The City-Guard.

O Muse! be kind, and dinna fash us
To flee awa beyont Parnassus,
Nor seek for Helicon to wash us,
That heath'nish spring!
Wi' Highland whisky scour our hawses,
And gar us sing!

(*fou* — drunk; *capernoity* — peevish, irritable; *dinna fash us* — don't vex us, make us angry; *scour our hawses* — clean out our throats)

Doubtful Wit and Wisdom

May those who love truly be always believed,
And those who deceive us be always deceived.

Here's to the men of all classes,
Who through lasses and glasses
Will make themselves asses!

I drink to the health of another,
And the other I drink to is he —
In the hope that he drinks to another,
And the other he drinks to is me.

Wit, or what passed for it in intoxicated company, was what the toast-makers of the eighteenth century mainly sought to display. The Scottish repertoire is full of verbal tricks to confuse the tipsy and make the toaster seem wise. Typical examples are:

A guid wife and health: a man's best wealth!

May we never want a friend to cheer us, or a bottle to cheer him!

Hard drinking of the kind that went on during The Enlightenment was rarely enjoyed by women. Predictably, therefore, sex, love and marriage were always popular topics — with toasts such as:

The dignity of the Fair Sex.

Success to the lover and joy to the beloved.

Days of peace and nights of pleasure!

Scotland Yet

Gae bring my guid auld harp aince mair;
Gae bring it free and fast,
For I maun sing anither sang
Ere a' my glee be past:
And trow ye as I sing, my lads,
The burthen o't shall be —
Auld Scotland's howes and Scotland's knowes,
And Scotland's hills for me!

I'll drink a cup to Scotland yet,
Wi' a' the honours three!

The thistle wags upon the fields
Where Wallace bore his blade,
That gave her foe-men's dearest build
To dye her auld grey plaid:
And, looking to the lift my lads,
He sang in doughty glee —
"Auld Scotland's right, and Scotland's might,
And Scotland's hills for me!"

Then drink a cup to Scotland yet,
Wi' a' the honours three!

(*gae* — go; *aince* — once; *maun* — must; *glee* — joy; *trow* — know, feel sure about; *howes and knowes* — hollows and knolls; *heath* — heather; *lo'e* — love; *Wallace* — Sir William Wallace, the "Father of Scottish nationhood")

Whisky

Then let us toast John Barleycorn,
Each man a glass in hand
And may his great prosperity
Ne'er fail in Old Scotland!

Whisky has been drunk in Scotland since time immemorial: a strong tradition holds that its manufacture was introduced from Ireland, and that it was brought to Ireland by St. Patrick, who came from what is now southern Scotland.

The earliest documentary reference to whisky appears in the Scottish Exchequer Rolls for 1494 —"eight bolls of malt to Friar John Cor wherewith to make aquavitae".

The name "whisky" derives from the Gaelic for *aquavitae* — *uisge beatha*: the Water of Life — but the term was not in general use in the Lowlands until the eighteenth century.

By the 1570s so much whisky was being produced for domestic consumption that there was a shortage of grain for making bread and bannocks but, until the eighteenth century, Scotland s "national" drinks were claret (for those who could afford it) and home-brewed ale, known as "two-penny ale" (or "tipenny").

Robert Burns refers to this in *Tam o'Shanter* (1790):

Inspiring, bold John Barleycorn,
What dangers thou canst make us scorn!
Wi' tipenny, we fear nae evil:
Wi' usquebae, we'll face the devil!

Balmoral-ity

Here's to the heath, the hill and the heather,
The bonnet, the plaid, the kilt and the feather!

Here's to the heroes that Scotland can boast,
May their names never dee —
That's the Heilan' Man's toast!

(dee — die)

Let's drink a drop o' barley bree,
Though moon and stars should blink thegither:
To each leaf lad wi' kilted knee,
And bonnie lass amang the heather.

(*bree* — drink, liquor)

Cloying sentimentality and tartan absurdity became identified
with Scotland during the late nineteenth century, promulgated
by music hall artists such as Harry Lauder. These toasts are
worthy only of picture post-cards illustrated with thistles and
Scottie dogs.

Such toasts do have provenance, however. An earlier,
Gaelic, version runs:

Tir nam beann, nan gleann, nan gaisach!

(i.e. To the land of the bens, the glens and the heroes!)

The Tartan

Here's to it.

The fighting sheen o'it;
The yellow, the green o'it;
The black, the red o'it;
Every thread o'it.
The fair have sighed for it;
The brave have died for it;
Foemen sought for it;
Heroes faught for it;
Honour the name o'it;
Drink to the fame o'it –
THE TARTAN.

This is a further example of Victorian sentimentality, wrong in every particular.

Tartan cloth has been worn by Gaels since time immemorial — there is a fragment of checked cloth in the Royal Scottish Museum, known as the "Falkirk Tartan", which dates from the third century A.D. — but the pattern of the cloth was not originally an expression of identity or membership of a clan. Plaids and bolts of cloth were looted during clan raids, and the smokey atmosphere that most clansfolk lived in will have ensured that their tartan's original colours became kippered. Tartan only became part of the definition of clanship after 1822.

A Gaelic Blessing

May the hill rise behind you,
And may the mountain be always over the crest;
And may the God that you believe in
Hold you in the palm of his hand.

There are several charming variations of this toast in Ireland as well as Scotland, such as:

May the Lord keep you in his hand,
And never close his fist too tight on you.

and

May the road rise to meet you;
May the wind be always at your back,
The sun shine warm upon your face,
The rain fall soft upon your fields.
And until we meet again,
May God hold you in the hollow of his hand.

Regimental Toasts

(The Royal Scots)

Slainte mhath, h-uile latha, na chi 'snach fhaic. Slainte!

(i.e. Good health, every day, whether I see you or not. Health!)

(Scots Guards)

Deoch slainte ne bhan Righ

(i.e. God's health to the King)

After he has played his *piobroch* at a regimental dinner, the Pipe Major receives a *quaich* (Gaelic for cup; a silver bowl, with a small handle on either side) of whisky from the Commanding Officer. He pronounces the regimental toast, drains the *quaich*, finishes with "*Slainte*", salutes and march out.

(St. Andrew's Night)

Gentlemen, let us drink in solemn silence
to the pious memory of our patron saint, St. Andrew

Most Scottish regiments celebrate St. Andrew's Night with a dinner. After the meal, the regimental *quaich* is carried round by the Colour Sergeant and presented to each officer in turn. The officer rises to receive the *quaich*, as do those on his either side (to protect him). He drinks, kisses the bottom of the *quaich* and passes it back to the Colour Sergeant, who continues round the table.

Here's Looking at You …

Here's to me and here's to you,
And if in the world
There was just us two —
And I could promise that nobody knew —
Would you?

This is a modern toast, but it echoes the original tradition of "toasting", which honoured the fair sex, often with innuendo.

Examples from the Scottish repertoire are numerous, some of them unprintable:

Virtuous desires and those desires gratified!

The maiden's blush, and a virgin of fifteen!

Love and opportunity!

Days of ease and nights of pleasure!

Old wine and young women!

Undoubtedly the most famous variation on this theme was Humphrey Bogart's toast in *Casablanca*:

Here's looking at you, kid.

Another touching variation on this is the (possibly Irish) Gaelic toast:

I look towards you,
And I gently smells your breath

The People of Scotland, and of the World

Jock Tamson's Bairns

Scots are all "Jock Tamson's Bairns" whatever their rank or degree, and by implication the expression embraces the people of the entire Earth.

The phrase has been in common use in Scotland since at least the early nineteenth century — one traveller in the West (1827) recorded: "when a company are (sic) sitting together, and a neighbour drops in, it is usual to welcome him thus: Come awa, we're a' John Tamson s bairns'." Another recorded (1847) the familiar welcome: Nae ceremony, we're a' Jock Tamson's bairns here".

The derivation of the term is obscure, although, interestingly, "Jock Tamson" was once a jocular name for whisky. The original meaning probably embraced a group united by common sentiment or purpose, but the contemporary meaning was made plain by Kate Rennie Archer, the poet, in 1934:

We're a' Jock Tamson's bairnies.
An' Jock Tamson? Weel — he's God.

Index